Cover

Supporting Operation JOINT ENDEAVOR, *a 1st Armored Division's Abrams tank moves into Bosnia-Herzegovina in late December 1995.*

CMH Pub 70-97-1

Introduction

Bosnia-Herzegovina was the scene for the most violent armed conflict in Europe since World War II. The collapse of the Berlin Wall in 1989 marked the end of the Soviet Empire and its forcible control of Eastern Europe. Even as the Soviet Union was breaking apart and its satellite states were shedding the vestiges of Communist rule, the nonaligned Socialist Federal Republic of Yugoslavia also showed cracks in its national structure. Comprised of six "republics" and two autonomous regions, Yugoslavia had created a favorable impression throughout the world as a model state with diverse ethnic groups. In spite of a historical legacy of ethnic conflicts, the country of the "South Slavs" could claim over forty years of peace and harmony. This way of life, however, changed in the last decade of the twentieth century.

In a complex series of diplomatic and political maneuvers, four of the six republics—Slovenia, Croatia, Bosnia-Herzegovina, and Macedonia—separated from Yugoslavia between 1991 and 1992. Each secession was contested, with the most horrific destruction and violence occurring in centrally located Bosnia-Herzegovina. At least half of the entire population—more than two million people—was directly affected by a civil war that lasted from April 1992 to November 1995. Efforts by the United Nations and the European Union were ignored, cease-fires were not honored, civilians were massacred, and entire villages were destroyed. The ethnic cleansing that ravaged the country defied any semblance of restraint or responsibility.

Spurred by U.S. leadership, a peace agreement was signed in December 1995 authorizing the North Atlantic Treaty Organization (NATO) to intervene. As called for in the agreement, the NATO Implementation Force consisting of 60,000 military personnel, one-third of them American, was to enforce the peace and to facilitate the reconstruction of the country. To this end, a total of three successive peace enforcement operations were undertaken: JOINT ENDEAVOR, JOINT GUARD, and JOINT FORGE.

Thousands of pages already have been printed about the civil war in Bosnia-Herzegovina. This brochure, written by R. Cody

Phillips of the U.S. Army Center of Military History, is not a complete picture of the course of events in that war-torn country, but it will provide the reader with an understanding of the U.S. Army's role and scope of activities in Operations JOINT ENDEAVOR, JOINT GUARD, and JOINT FORGE. I hope this absorbing account, with its list of further readings, will stimulate additional study and reflection.

JOHN S. BROWN
Brigadier General, USA (Ret.)
Chief of Military History

Bosnia-Herzegovina

The U.S. Army's Role in Peace Enforcement Operations, 1995–2004

Civil war in Bosnia-Herzegovina erupted in April 1992. Over the next three and a half years between 140,000 and 250,000 people had been killed. At least four out of every five deaths were noncombatants. While an unknown number had been wounded or maimed—many from the thousands of land mines that saturated the country—the horror did not stop there. Perhaps as many as 12,000 women were raped, and 520,000 Bosnians found themselves homeless. Ethnic cleansing created over 1.3 million refugees, many of whom had fled to other countries or were trying desperately to escape the fighting and poverty that engulfed the region. Dozens of diplomatic initiatives and temporary truces failed before a U.S.-brokered agreement in late 1995, the Dayton Peace Accords, finally ended the fighting and permitted U.S. military forces to enter the country as part of the North Atlantic Treaty Organization (NATO) international force charged with the responsibility of enforcing the peace.

Sadly, by 1998, three years after the fighting had ended officially, seemingly irreconcilable differences still characterized the former warring factions. While accompanying a small patrol in a multiethnic area near Brcko, a battalion command sergeant major encountered a young Bosnian Serb who—with all the candor and innocence of his twelve years—asked "when the Americans were going to leave" so that he and his friends "could start killing each other again." It was a stark reminder of the critical importance of the U.S. Army in Bosnia-Herzegovina and what made the Army's mission so vital, yet so difficult, in the ensuing peace enforcement operations JOINT ENDEAVOR, JOINT GUARD, and JOINT FORGE.

Strategic Setting

Bosnia is located in the southeastern region of Europe commonly referred to as the Balkans. The country, which includes the large medieval duchy of Herzegovina, is slightly larger than

AUSTRIA

HUNGARY

Balaton

Slovenia
○ Ljubljana

○ Zagreb

Croatia

Vojvo
(Autonomou
of Ser

○
Novi S

Bosnia–Herzegovina

◉
SARAJEVO

Montenegro

A D R I A T I C   S E A

○
Podgorica

ITALY

ALB.

YUGOSLAVIA

March 1991

—·—·— Republic Boundary

0   100 Miles
0   100   Kilometers

Map 1

the state of Tennessee. Prior to the outbreak of civil war in 1992 Bosnia-Herzegovina was one of six republics that formed the larger nation of Yugoslavia (*Map 1*), and only eight years earlier its capital, Sarajevo, was the site for the 1984 Winter Olympics. Prewar images of Bosnia usually depict either picturesque rural settings reminiscent of late-nineteenth century Europe or cosmopolitan multiethnic towns that reflect a blend of Turkish and European history.

Notwithstanding the pastoral images and pacific urbanity of prewar Bosnia, the region had a turbulent history that dated as far back as the first century. The thirteenth-century Great Schism that formally separated Roman Catholic Christianity and Eastern Orthodox Christianity increased tensions in the region as both churches, relying respectively on monarchs in the West and the Byzantine emperor in the East, attempted to extend their influence over and control of the Balkans. A fledgling Bosnian kingdom appeared in the fourteenth century, but it barely survived one hundred years before being overwhelmed by the Turkish Ottoman Empire. For the next four hundred years Bosnia was a province of the Muslim rulers in Istanbul, and many Bosnians converted to Islam. During the Turkish dominance of the Balkan region significant numbers of ethnic nationals migrated to neighboring lands, forming minority enclaves. Migrants from Serbia tended to form the largest of this group in Bosnia and Croatia.Following a Russian campaign in the Balkans and the subsequent defeat of the Turks, the Congress of Berlin in 1878 placed Bosnia-Herzegovina under the control of the Austro-Hungarian Empire.This action frustrated Russian ambitions in the Balkans and failed to consider the nationalistic aspirations of the indigenous population. In Bosnia the populace tended to align by its ethnic and religious allegiances, with Slovenes and Croats associating with the Catholic West (usually Italy and Austria), Serbs identifying with the Russians and the Orthodox East, and Bosnian Muslims favoring the Islamic Turks. Although tension existed among these ethnic groups, their greater concern was to be freed of the dominating influence of the imperial powers that surrounded them. The Austrian mandate triggered a Bosnian Muslim revolt that was ruthlessly suppressed—150,000 Bosnians died. A Serbian rebellion followed, and this too was put down.These two Balkan uprisings on the eve of World War I effectively neutralized further Turkish influence in the Balkans, as well as led to a larger and more aggressive Serbia.The assassination of the heir to the Austro-Hungarian throne by a Bosnian Serb—a Serbian nationalist who resided in Austrian-occupied Bosnia—sparked the outbreak of World War I. Serbia, allied with Russia, valiantly fought the Austrians in a conflict that saw almost half of the young males in Serbia killed or wounded. The end of the war and the breakup of the Austro-Hungarian Empire brought about the arbitrary unification of the Slovenes, Croats, Serbs, and other ethnic minorities in the region under a conglomerate kingdom to be known as Yugoslavia (meaning *South Slavs*).

A depressed economy, ethnic tensions, and both external and internal political intrigue made the young Kingdom of Yugoslavia a fragile entity even before the outbreak of World War II. German forces occupied Yugoslavia in April 1941, and the ensuing occupation acerbated the divisions within the fledgling nation. The two leading Yugoslavian partisan forces, ostensibly organized to fight the Germans, spent inordinate time and resources fighting each other. Other ethnic groups affiliated with the Germans or their Italian allies and often fought against their partisan countrymen. By 1945 an estimated 1.7 million Yugoslavians had been killed in the internecine strife, representing over 11 percent of the prewar population.

Despite this incredible loss of life and significant damage to the country's infrastructure, people rallied to a new and reconstructed Yugoslavia—this one organized as a socialist federal republic under President Tito (Josip Broz). For thirty-five years Tito's firm control over the polyglot state subordinated ethnic rivalries to a pan-Yugoslavian ethos. Although ethnic enclaves remained scattered throughout the country, particularly in the republics of Croatia and Bosnia, there was free and unrestricted movement among the population. Within Bosnia, ethnic Croats and Serbs often formed small majorities in the countryside and villages, with the former usually found in the western and southern sections and the latter customarily living in the northern and eastern parts. Bosnian Muslims tended to dominate the large towns and cities. Mixed marriages became relatively common. By the late 1980s 30 percent of the marriages in the urban communities of Bosnia were among couples of different ethnic backgrounds. Indeed, especially in larger towns and cities in Bosnia, it was not uncommon to find Croatians, Muslims, and Serbs all working in the same factory, attending the same school, or living on the same street. In fact, Bosnia's multiethnic heritage was one of its most prominent characteristics. By 1990 ethnic Croats could be found living throughout roughly 70 percent of the state, while Bosnian Muslims and Bosnian Serbs—usually intermingled in communities—occupied almost 95 percent of Bosnia-Herzegovina. Population estimates at the time indicated that Muslims comprised over 44 percent, and still increasing; Serbs, slightly more than 31 percent; and ethnic Croats, 17 percent.

Tito died in 1980, with Yugoslavia remaining under Communist rule for another ten years. However, the collapse of communism throughout Eastern Europe and the disintegration of the Soviet Union had a profound effect on the country's future. As the Communist Party lost its grip on the Balkan country, the individual republics began to assert more control over their internal affairs. Concerned that growing Serbian influence in Yugoslavia might affect their autonomy, the republics began to seriously consider independence. Slovenia, the northernmost republic, was the first to separate in June 1991. A perfunctory week-long "war" followed, during which the Yugoslav Army tried to reassert national authority in the region. The almost bloodless conflict quickly ended, and the Yugoslav government accepted Slovene independence.

Very few ethnic Serbs resided in Slovenia, and this situation influenced the Serbian leadership in Belgrade to accept Slovene secession. In the case of neighboring Croatia, however, where rising Croatian patriotism clashed with local Serbian nationalists, the response was different. When several attempts to achieve a political resolution failed, armed conflict erupted in August 1991 and continued intermittently for the next four years. During the struggle ethnic Serbs residing in Croatia, aided by elements of the Yugoslav Army, seized large tracts of land and held them until Croatia forcibly reclaimed the lost territory in 1995.

In an effort to stem the fighting in Croatia, the United Nations (UN) imposed an arms embargo on all the republics of Yugoslavia in September 1991. The following year the United Nations Protection Force (UNPROFOR), created in April 1992 as the UN's second largest peacekeeping contingent, arrived to enforce a cease-fire among the combatants, but the events were moving too rapidly for the UN to control. The force never exceeded 10,000 personnel scattered through Bosnia and Croatia. As one observer later noted, "UNPROFOR was an army . . . without a clear mission, and almost powerless in the middle of a mess."

Once the European countries recognized the independence of Slovenia and Croatia in January 1992, Bosnian leaders realized that they too could achieve independence—if only to avoid being dominated by neighboring Serbia. In March, in a referendum that was boycotted by the Bosnian Serb minority, an overwhelming majority of the voters chose to separate from Yugoslavia. Recognizing that implementation of this electoral decision might lead to conflicts similar to those that already had occurred in Slovenia and Croatia, the Bosnian political leadership tried to reach a political resolution with the Yugoslav government in Belgrade. But the Bosnian Serb minority proved adamantly opposed to such an initiative. On the afternoon of 6 April a "peace and unity" demonstration in the Bosnian capital of Sarajevo was disrupted when Bosnian Serbs fired shots into the crowd and killed several demonstrators. The violence marked the beginning of civil war in Bosnia.

Armed largely with weapons received from the Yugoslav Army, Bosnian Serbs seized parts of Bosnia and expelled the non-Serbian population of ethnic Croats and Muslims. Families that delayed their departure or resisted often were killed or had their homes and property destroyed. The central government in Sarajevo was slow to respond to these initial outrages, and the Bosnian Serbs quickly created their own country, the *Republika Srpska* (Serb Republic), out of the territory carved from Bosnia. At the same time, the UN Security Council extended the UNPROFOR mandate to include Bosnia-Herzegovina. Momentum was with the Bosnian Serbs, who aggressively prosecuted the war relying on overwhelming firepower, Yugoslav Army assistance, and the fear instilled in other minorities.

Sarajevo was quickly surrounded, and eventually Bosnian Serb forces occupied nearly 70 percent of the country. In a wave of ethnic cleansing not seen in Europe since World War II hundreds of thousands of civilians were forcibly removed from their homes, and thousands more were killed. Repeated UN and European attempts to establish and maintain a cease-fire or negotiate an end to the hostilities failed. When the UN secretary general arrived in Sarajevo for a high-profile visit and promotion of a new peace initiative in early 1993, protestors greeted him with placards that read: "Stop defending us your way. We are getting exterminated." By 1994 reports of mass murders and rapes, incredible property damage, and a surging refugee population were shocking testimonies to the unsuccessful political and diplomatic efforts to end this civil war.

U.S. policy had initially favored the survival of Yugoslavia as a unitary state. Looking at the rapid dissolution of the former Soviet Union and its attendant problems with multiple fledgling states, U.S. leaders feared that a similar situation would destabilize the Balkans. At first, however, they were content to allow the European Community to handle the deteriorating situation. This would be "the hour of Europe."

American hopes for a continental solution proved unrealistic. The European Community—soon to become the European Union—could not reach a consensus on the appropriate course of action. Deferring to the UN to exercise oversight for protecting the civilian population and negotiating a peaceful resolution appeared to be the only solution, but UNPROFOR had proven too small and lightly armed for the tasks. Moreover, its exceedingly restrictive rules of engagement and cumbersome command structure had prevented UN peacekeepers from stopping even the most egregious acts of violence. In some cases UNPROFOR commanders were bullied into silence or retreat, and some UNPROFOR detachments even became hostages when the European Union attempted to take more forceful action.

Paralyzed with fears of an escalating conflict and frustrated by repeated failures to stem the fighting, UNPROFOR allowed the war in Bosnia to rage for three years. In the end, the peacekeeping force was barely able to defend itself and protect the humanitarian relief coming into the country. Further dampening any enthusiasm for a more robust response were NATO's estimates that somewhere between 150,000 and 460,000 military personnel, at least half to be American, would be necessary to stop the war and reverse all Bosnian Serb gains.

As the war in Bosnia ground on through 1993 and 1994, a variety of issues complicated any effective U.S. response to the unfolding tragedy. The possibility of a massive American military presence in south-central Europe seemed reminiscent of what had occurred a generation earlier in Southeast Asia. More recently, the tragic losses of special operations soldiers in Somalia tempered committing others to a conflict with blurred front lines, an imprecise mission, and an uncertain enemy. The European Union insisted on pursuing diplomatic solutions, unless the United States was willing to commit military force on the ground—a course of action that neither the American public nor Congress was eager to support. Less significant, but troubling nonetheless, Muslim fundamentalists from the Middle East—mujahideen—had infiltrated Bosnia to add a new mix to the increasingly confused contest. Bosnia was, in the words of U.S. Secretary of State Warren Christopher, "the problem from hell."

The United States and the European Union—particularly the United Kingdom and France—could not agree on a uniform policy and resolution to the crisis in Bosnia, creating a severe strain on the NATO alliance. A significant portion of the UNPROFOR personnel came from NATO's European Union members. Although they were anxious for the fighting in the Balkans to stop, they were reluctant to engage in any activity that might jeopardize their soldiers already in the region. Conversely, the United States, with no military personnel at the time in Bosnia, advocated more forceful military responses to Serbian provocations. The U.S. position came to be characterized as "lift and strike": lift the UN arms embargo on Bosnia, and use NATO airpower to enforce the no-fly zone over the country and launch punitive strikes against Bosnian Serb military targets. The UN, which asserted a military presence in the area through its protection force, did not have aircraft to enforce the no-fly zone over Bosnia, so it accepted the offer of NATO aircraft to perform this task. But the heavily layered and cautious UN command insisted on retaining final approval for all NATO combat flights over Bosnia.

Initially, U.S. policy settled on a middle course of easing the tensions in the NATO alliance and using aggressive diplomacy to contain the war in Bosnia and preserve its territorial integrity. The effort was short-lived. In 1994 NATO launched limited air strikes, sardonically called "pinpricks," but they did not stem the Bosnian Serb offensives. The first combat action in NATO's history occurred in late February, when U.S. Air Force aircraft shot down four Bosnian Serb planes that violated the no-fly zone. Another action followed six weeks later on 10 April, when NATO aircraft engaged ground targets in retaliation for Bosnian Serb attacks on a UN safe area. But these isolated air strikes accomplished little. The cumbersome approval process mitigated both their effectiveness and timeliness, and the willingness of both Bosnian Serbs and Bosnian Muslims to use UN military personnel as hostages or human shields further complicated the use of NATO airpower. Worse still, the threat of NATO air strikes failed to prevent the horrific massacre of 8,000 Bosnian men and boys in Srebrenica in the summer of 1995.

The court of world opinion already had been tilting against the Bosnian Serbs. The Srebrenica massacre ended all doubts. In the following weeks a rebuilt Croatian military launched a campaign to retake lost territory from Croatian and Bosnian Serbs. Concurrently, Croatian Bosnians, concentrated in central and western Bosnia, and Bosnian Muslims formed a military alliance and initiated a counteroffensive against the Bosnian Serbs. In a series of battles throughout the summer the Bosnian Serbs lost large sections of territory. In mid-August 1995 a special U.S. envoy and team began a series of negotiations among the heads of the different warring factions, with the intention of bringing about a cease-fire and a permanent peace in the area. Despite being pressed from all directions, the Bosnian Serbs were obdurate. When a Bosnian Serb artillery round fired into Sarajevo killed thirty-seven civilians and wounded eighty-five others, the UN command acquiesced to NATO's insistence on a sustained air campaign against the Bosnian Serbs.

On 30 August NATO launched Operation DELIBERATE FORCE. Over sixty NATO aircraft from eight countries, plus British and French artillery, hit preplanned targets scattered around Bosnia. Thereafter, sustained bombing began and continued until 20 September, when Bosnian Serbs agreed to remove their heavy artillery from around besieged Sarajevo. The U.S. diplomatic initiative, the Croatian-Bosnian counteroffensive, and the aggressive air campaign all combined to bring the Serbians, Croatians, and Bosnian Muslims together for peace talks that were held at Wright-

Patterson Air Force Base, near Dayton, Ohio.

U.S. diplomats arranged a tenuous cease-fire among all the warring factions in October, on the eve of the Dayton peace talks. After three weeks of intense negotiations the representatives of the former warring factions approved an agreement on 21 November, which was subsequently formalized in the formal General Framework Agreement for Peace in Paris on 14 December. Among its many provisions was the establishment of the NATO Implementation Force (IFOR), which would include U.S. military personnel deployed to Bosnia-Herzegovina (*Map 2*) to facilitate compliance with the Dayton Accords and to maintain the cease-fire.

Defining the IFOR mission was not easy. The tasks required clearly specified limitations and specific objectives. Sensitive to the qualified congressional support and the vicissitudes of public opinion, U.S. negotiators charted a careful course to avoid the ubiquitous "mission creep" that beleaguered the American experience in Somalia and the open-ended U.S. involvement in Southeast Asia. Ultimately, IFOR was charged with several major tasks: enforce the cease-fire, control air space over Bosnia, separate the former warring factions, and supervise boundaries along zones of separation. Military movements would be monitored along key routes, and joint military commissions were to be formed as consultative bodies among all the parties to the peace agreement. Some of the UN forces already present in Bosnia would be transferred to IFOR; the rest were to be withdrawn.

The 57,000 military members of IFOR, 20,000 of them Americans, were under NATO command. For operational purposes and for securing different areas of Bosnia-Herzegovina, NATO organized IFOR into three subordinate commands—Multinational Division (North), Multinational Division (Southwest), and Multinational Division (Southeast). The U.S. area of operations would be in Multinational Division (North)—MND (N). Within the American sector other nations supplying military personnel included Turkey, Denmark, Estonia, Finland, Latvia, Lithuania, Norway, Poland, and Sweden. Almost as an affirmation of the end of the Cold War, a Russian military force would also participate with the NATO forces in bringing peace to Bosnia.

Preparations

The U.S. military had a small presence in the region even prior to the official deployment of ground forces to Bosnia in December 1995. Prior to the initial NATO air strikes on Bosnian Serb targets in 1994, U.S. Air Force and Army personnel were providing humanitarian aid in airlifts of food and other supplies to Croatia and Bosnia under the auspices of Operation PROVIDE PROMISE, which had begun in July 1992. Five months later a mobile army surgical hospital deployed to Zagreb, Croatia. Originally there to support UN military personnel and relief agencies, it eventually treated over 6,000 civilian patients. Months later, British and U.S. special operations personnel quietly entered Bosnia to improve communications capabilities among the UN forces and reconnoiter possible military targets.

Planning for a possible deployment of U.S. Army ground forces to Bosnia began in April 1992 soon after the war started. That same year U.S. Army Europe (USAREUR) units started focusing their training on stability operations. The process became more deliberate by the summer of 1994, when it appeared that UNPROFOR might be withdrawn because of the deteriorating situation in Bosnia. By that time USAREUR had prepared a draft operational plan and identified specific participating units, including up to nine combat brigades entering from multiple avenues to rescue the UN forces and stabilize the region.

Among U.S. military personnel, such planning was neither a surprise nor much of a secret. As one platoon sergeant assigned to

USAREUR since 1993 had opined: "It's always been one of those things—we've been training to come to Bosnia-Herzegovina for as long as I've been here." Comparable training and preparations also occurred among Army Reserve units in the United States. By early summer of 1995 some kind of U.S. Army involvement seemed certain, and individual units began preparing for specific scenarios, particularly with stability operations training and exercises involving multinational headquarters. In the words of one 1st Armored Division staff officer, "This thing just didn't sneak up on us; we saw it coming a long way out."

Mission rehearsal exercises (MRE) began in June 1995, with over 1,000 USAREUR, U.S. Air Force Europe, and U.S. European Command (EUCOM) personnel participating in MRE Mountain Shield I. The MRE concept was designed to anticipate contingency operations in other regions of the world and integrate all training and exercises to compliment preparations for possible future missions. MRE Mountain Shield II, held three months later, involved over 4,200 personnel and focused on a variety of operations in which a U.S. joint task force had the mission of extracting a UN protection force from a fictitious country. It was understood that Bosnia-Herzegovina was the country in question and that the 1st Armored Division would be the lead combat element for the mission. With the imminent implementation of a cease-fire in Bosnia and the expected start of peace talks in Dayton, preparations for a deployment of Army personnel shifted into high gear. Leaves were canceled, and USAREUR received authorization from the Department of the Army to extend personnel in their present duty assignments while accelerating the arrival of newly assigned soldiers in order to bring individual units up to full strength.

MRE Mountain Eagle 95, which included over 10,000 personnel from the 1st Armored Division and the V Corps, began on 12 October and continued through most of November. In this multi-faceted exercise the projected scenario shifted so that units and individual personnel received training in peacekeeping operations and negotiation techniques. The organizational element to be deployed in this contingency operation was designated Task Force Eagle, and every soldier within the task force was required to be trained and certified in five core categories: rules of engagement, mine awareness, negotiations, patrolling, and checkpoint operations. Additional training focused on stability and information operations, internal security and force protection measures, and working with joint military commissions. Several months later, as his tour in Bosnia was concluding, a company commander reflected on how well his unit had functioned and credited the success to the training done before the deployment: It was "right on the money," which "really paid us big dividends."

In spite of all the training and preparation for a possible mission in Bosnia-Herzegovina, significant problems appeared during the actual deployment—and most of them were either unpredictable or beyond the control of military planners. Political decisions altered the anticipated flow of personnel and logistical support from bases in Germany to the Balkans and generally forced more combat forces into the theater of operations ahead of their requisite support. This unbalance was complicated by an unexpected rail strike in neighboring France, which restricted the availability of railcars that were needed to transport major equipment items and bulk supplies. The reduction in transportation assets was further exacerbated by a paucity of storage facilities to pre-position supplies and equipment. Some deploying units were understrength, which increased the workload for personnel in those organizations. Traversing non-NATO countries in a military deployment and contending with the approach of the holiday season also complicated the movement to Bosnia. Just as Task Force Eagle was about to enter the war-torn country in force, the Balkan winter set in. Ice, snow, knee-deep mud, and swollen rivers added more delays to the deployment.

To surmount several unforeseen problems, American soldiers adopted unusual solutions. When some commanders found themselves separated from their units while reconnoitering staging areas and routes into Bosnia, they relied upon personal cell phones or other units to maintain contact with their own organizations. In another case transportation companies used credit cards to pay for fuel and lodging for the three-day 1,000-mile trip from Germany to the border of Bosnia. Looking over the variety of ad hoc and stopgap solutions employed, one brigade commander concluded that the sheer determination and creativity of individual soldiers were key factors in completing the deployment.

The most significant obstacle was crossing the Sava River. The longest watercourse in the former Yugoslavia, it constituted the northern border between Bosnia-Herzegovina and Croatia. December was regarded as a high-water period for the Sava, and Mother Nature truly challenged the Army engineers who began bridging the waterway on 20 December. Days later the river overflowed its banks and flooded parts of the American camp, forcing the engineers to suspend their work. By using all assets in theater to construct the largest pontoon bridge since World War II, commanders of the lead units crossed the Sava on the twenty-ninth in a civilian ferry to reconnoiter what was to become the U.S. area of operations MND (N). During the return trip, however, the ferry had mechanical difficulties, and portions of the pontoon bridge had to be dismantled during a snowstorm in order to extract the stranded Americans. But despite all difficulties, on the thirty-first, with the bridge finally completed, an M1A2 Abrams tank from the 1st Armored Division's 1st Squadron, 1st Cavalry, led the American contingent across the Sava River into Bosnia-Herzegovina for Operation JOINT ENDEAVOR.

Operation JOINT ENDEAVOR

Since the outbreak of civil war in Bosnia-Herzegovina, the many cease-fires had been violated—sometimes within hours of being implemented. The legacy of numerous unprovoked attacks on UNPROFOR personnel also was troubling. Unsure how the former warring factions—Bosnian Serbs, Croatians, and Bosnian Muslims—might respond to the U.S. military presence, Task Force Eagle's intent was to demonstrate overwhelming power and resolve in order to discourage any hostile response. Columns of armored vehicles thundered down narrow dirt roads and dozens of attack helicopters flew overhead, all demonstrating that the present cease-fire would be enforced and the provisions of the Dayton Accords would be implemented. As one 1st Armored Division staff officer later observed, "The task force deployed with sufficient force to annihilate the factional armies. Clearly, this was instrumental in ensuring their full cooperation and compliance."

Officially, the deployment of U.S. forces began on 2 December 1995 and concluded on 14 February 1996. By the time that the movement was completed, over 24,000 soldiers and 12,000 major equipment items had been moved in support of Operation JOINT ENDEAVOR. The heart of the U.S. contingent consisted of the 1st and 2d Brigades, 1st Armored Division (*Chart*), which included thirteen combat support and combat service support formations: the 1st Squadron, 1st Cavalry; the 3d Battalion, 5th Cavalry; the 4th Battalion (-), 67th Armor; the 2d Battalion, 3d Field Artillery; the 23d Engineer Battalion; the 501st Support Battalion; the 4th Battalion, 12th Infantry; the 2d Battalion (attached), 15th Infantry; the 2d Battalion (-), 68th Armor; the 3d Squadron (attached), 4th

Chart—Organization of Task Force Eagle

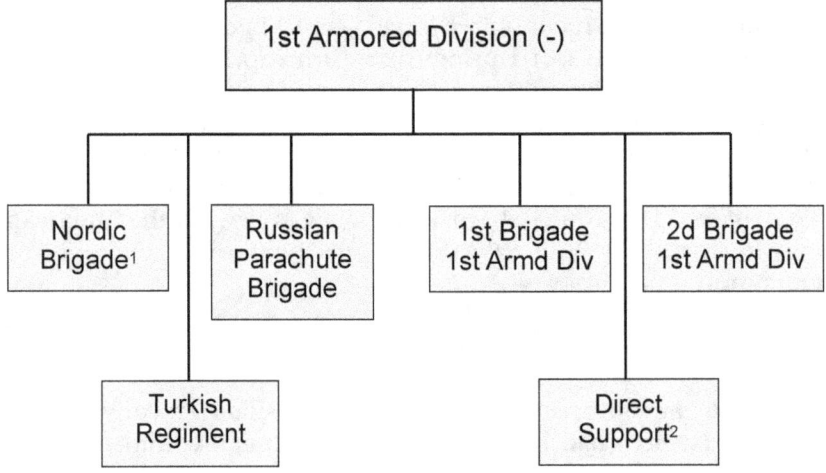

[1]Consisted of infantry, mechanized, military police, transportation, and engineer units from seven nations.

[2]Consisted of artillery, combat support, and combat service support units drawn mostly (but not exclusively) from the 1st Armored Division and spread between Bosnia and Hungary.

Cavalry; the 4th Battalion, 29th Field Artillery; the 40th Engineer Battalion; and the 47th Support Battalion. Several smaller companies, batteries, and detachments of various units also were included in this force package. To keep the force levels within prescribed limits, the USAREUR (Forward) headquarters and major logistical facilities were positioned in neighboring Hungary and Croatia. The initial deployment required 409 trains and 7,340 railcars, 507 buses, 1,700 tractor-trailers, and 1,358 aircraft sorties.

Despite thorough training and a deliberate approach to this peace enforcement operation, Task Force Eagle suffered its first casualty even before the main contingent was able to cross the Sava River into Bosnia. On 30 December a soldier from the 127th Military Police Company ran over an antitank mine with his vehicle and was seriously injured. The MPs had been conducting a reconnaissance to mark the routes for the armored division to follow to its cantonments and checkpoints in Bosnia. The episode underscored the dangerous environment that U.S. forces soon would be occupying.

Ten days earlier, on 20 December, the UN formally relinquished control to NATO. Leading the U.S. Army forces for Operation Joint Endeavor was V Corps commander Lt. Gen. John N. Abrams, dual-hatted as the deputy commanding general of USAREUR (Forward). The ground component commander for U.S. forces in Bosnia, Task Force Eagle, was 1st Armored Division commander Maj. Gen. William L. Nash, who situated his headquarters in the Bosnian city of Tuzla in the center of MND (N). Most of the UNPROFOR personnel already in Bosnia simply changed their uniforms (usually the UN light blue helmet and armband to the soldier's national uniform) and either relocated or remained in place as part of the new IFOR. Thus, the French forces shifted to the south, the British forces shifted to the west, the Russian and Turkish forces remained in the northeast area of Bosnia under the jurisdiction of the MND (N).

The initial operational task was to separate the former warring factions into their respective areas and establish a zone of separation. By then, combat activity in MND (N) was largely static, with opposing forces fighting from fixed positions. Barbed wire entanglements around entrenchments, roadblocks, bunkers, and minefields saturated the area. Most of the buildings in and around the zone of separation had already been destroyed or extensively damaged. It was an austere environment, with one brigade commander affirming that the potholes were larger than the roads.

Task Force Eagle quickly set about its peace enforcement mission. After securing the former UNPROFOR cantonment sites as well as others, individual units began to assert their control over the region through checkpoints on roads and bridges and aggressive patrolling. The American soldiers found the former warring factions and the ethnic groups exhausted by three years of continuous bloodshed and the populace generally docile but most appreciative. In particular, those on patrol were offered small tokens of gratitude in the form of food and drink, but such gifts were usually declined for security reasons.

A number of isolated and spontaneous incidents challenged the American soldiers, but the outcomes demonstrated both their restraint and the quality of their training and discipline. For instance, soon after starting on a routine patrol, an intoxicated civilian blocked a Bradley fighting vehicle and brandished two firearms, which he began firing wildly at the armored personnel carrier. The vehicle commander simply closed his hatch and waited for the civilian to exhaust his ammunition, and then bystanders subdued him and carried him away. Random gunfire sometimes was

Typical U.S. Army checkpoint in Bosnia-Herzegovina

directed at U.S. troops or equipment, but none of the shots hit the intended targets. Once a hand grenade was thrown at an armored vehicle, but it caused no damage. Other episodes occurred, for example, a rock or an empty bottle being hurled at a passing patrol, but they were few in number. As the weeks went by, patrol operations and checkpoints became a common activity performed by IFOR and casually observed by the local civilians. In time, fighting the tedium and staying alert weighed heavily on most of the U.S. forces in MDN (N).

But all the former warring factions were not idle. Soon after U.S. troops in Task Force Eagle had established their checkpoints and settled into an expected routine, a two-truck convoy of Bosnian Serbs challenged an isolated outpost by trying to speed past the American guards. The first truck slipped past the checkpoint, but the second truck was stopped. The U.S. Army sergeant ordered the twenty-two armed Bosnian Serb soldiers out of the truck. In perfect English, one of the Serbs said: "I'll kill you." Calmly, the sergeant pointed his rifle at the speaker and replied, "I don't think you will," and repeated his order. By then, the other four U.S. troops at the checkpoint arrived to guard the Bosnian Serbs, while the sergeant collected two-dozen firearms and ammunition.

In another early incident a Task Force Eagle patrol observed a man carrying an automatic rifle inside the zone of separation. The patrol approached the individual to confiscate his weapon, but noted that several other armed personnel were in a nearby house watching the patrol. The patrol leader immediately radioed his headquarters, and within minutes several IFOR armored vehicles and a senior officer with interpreters arrived on the scene, while attack helicopters hovered in the distance. This synchronized tactical response to a potentially volatile situation was sufficient to permit all of the civilians to be disarmed peacefully. Then too, the generally decentralized troop distribution facilitated the quick concentration of necessary force at trouble spots.

Episodes like this were typical of the early phases of Operation JOINT ENDEAVOR. What made them especially sensitive and significant was the near-certainty that they could easily escalate and spin out of control. In a stability or peace enforcement operation, a successful mission was credited to commanders and their personnel who did not have to resort to force of arms. Every nonlethal option to achieve a desired end was encouraged, while convincing the opposing force that implementation of overwhelming combat power was imminent. Of note, the small-unit leaders—noncommissioned and company-grade officers—were making these decisions.

At least thirty patrols occurred every day, with three platoons on alert as a quick-reaction force that could be committed to respond to any exigency that might arise. On infrequent occasions gunfire would be exchanged between the former warring factions, for example, snipers firing across the zone of separation and then scampering away before U.S. troops or aircraft could arrive on the scene. In other cases civilians of one ethnic background might accidentally stray into a different ethnic area, and U.S. forces would be called in to rescue the hapless individuals. Each crisis had strategic, operational, and tactical implications. In a world dominated by instant communications, any violent flare-up or any mistake could significantly affect national policies and the fate of the peace enforcement operation in Bosnia.

More complex examples abounded and not all ended happily. The Dayton Accords clearly specified limitations on carrying arms within the zone of separation or crossing into another ethnic area without coordinating such movements through IFOR. Thus, when seven armed Bosnian Muslims found inside the borders of the Serb Republic tried to surrender to U.S. forces, they were disarmed and transferred to Bosnian Serb police, who believed that these men were responsible for the murder of some Bosnian Serbs a few days earlier. The men claimed to be survivors of the Serbian massacre in Srebrenica, but the evidence was inconclusive. The action complied with treaty requirements, but the International Red Cross disputed the Army's decision. General Nash immediately sent a senior officer to the Bosnian Serb police station, along with a small team of observers from the UN and the recently constituted International Police Task Force (IPTF). Their stay was cut short when a hostile crowd gathered outside the station. The IPTF inspectors returned the following day, only to be denied access to the Muslim prisoners. The prisoners were transferred a few days later to another city 30 miles away, where another IPTF inspector was able to visit the Muslims and report that they had been severely beaten and tortured. The final fate of the prisoners remained unknown to American authorities.

Within the context of the larger operation, the episode was minor, but it also was characteristic of the problems surrounding Operation Joint Endeavor. On any given day U.S. forces could encounter a variety of isolated and unrelated issues, and there was no predicting which ones might suddenly surface as an international incident. A sergeant or lieutenant at a remote checkpoint was fully aware of the potential ramifications of every decision that he made.

Military authorities constantly worked at defusing potential problems and ensuring proper civil-military coordination. Although zone-of-separation security was the most visible element of Task Force Eagle's activities, commanders also engaged in political affairs and economic recovery. To improve the local economy and to encourage positive interchange among the indigenous ethnic groups, one brigade commander created the Arizona Market—an open-air commercial enterprise for Bosnian Muslim and Bosnian Serb businesses. The joint military commissions demanded significant investments of time just to keep the former warring factions talking to each other.

A recurring problem for the U.S. forces in Bosnia was the constant animosity between the ethnic and religious groups. Army personnel often noted the deliberate destruction of nonmilitary targets—such as private homes, churches, and mosques—that occurred during the war. So it came as no surprise that these tensions continued when, in accordance with the Dayton Accords, some Bosnian Muslims, or "Bosniacs," tried to resettle in areas that they had occupied before the war began. One volatile episode began in late April 1996 and continued through the following month. Muslim civilians crossed the zone of separation and entered Bosnia Serb territory, with the intention of either visiting family grave sites or reoccupying their former homes. They had not gone far when armed Serbs met them. Shots were exchanged, with one Muslim killed. Some of the Muslim civilians panicked and ran through a marked minefield, where six were injured. A reinforced armored column from the 3d Squadron, 4th Cavalry, quickly arrived at the site before the situation could spin out of control. The U.S. soldiers disarmed the Serbians and escorted the Muslims out of Serb territory. In the following weeks additional weapons and munitions were confiscated from both ethnic groups as Muslims tried to enter the Serbian side of the zone of separation and Bosnian Serbs continued to block their efforts.

The rapid and resolute response to this episode, as well as many like it, prevented such situations from spiraling into more serious problems. Sometimes, however, the operations were not so seamless. In November 1996 a company of American infantrymen, working with Russian paratroopers in MND (N), stopped a small group of Muslims from provoking neighboring Serbs, making the group leave the zone of separation near the burned-out village of Gajevi. But hours later as many as 600 Bosnian Muslims suddenly gathered and started moving toward Serb territory. Paramilitary Serbian forces quickly arrived to block their route of advance after some shots were fired at Serbian homes. Familiar with the now-predictable IFOR response to such provocations, this clearly was an orchestrated political event that was designed to attract media attention. In view of the planned rotation of U.S. forces, the incident also may have been prompted to exploit the temporary vacuum engendered by the change in forces and the concurrent changes of command.

The Bosnian Muslims, claiming their right to resettle in their former homeland as formally acknowledged in the Dayton Accords, refused to leave. In response, the Serbian forces started to advance on the crowd, and the senior American commander warned them to halt or be shot. His action appeared to end the confrontation, with both sides eventually dispersing. Nevertheless, in the same region on 12 November, the Bosnian Serbs and Muslims exchanged random gunfire, resulting in the death of at least one Muslim. By now, IFOR personnel had determined that the Muslims were carrying weapons into the zone of separation and had an undocumented arsenal nearby. Two companies of tanks and armored personnel carriers, with trucks and support personnel, launched a predawn raid on the arsenal site and confiscated over 1,000 firearms. As they were leaving, a hostile Muslim crowd gathered to block the American forces from withdrawing. When negotiations with the agitators failed, the task force commander tried various nonlethal means of dispersing the crowd. Nothing worked. Eventually, the U.S. soldiers disembarked from their vehicles and forced a path through the crowd for themselves and their vehicles. Individual soldiers were kicked, punched, and spat on. When subjected to a flurry of rocks and debris, they raised their firearms and pointed them toward the pressing crowd, which immediately began to thin and disperse. Although there were no casualties, the incident highlighted how easily a situation could become uncontrollable and how tense the situation was—even after months of an enforced peace.

It seemed that every military organization among the former warring factions maintained a weapons cache or small arsenal. One of the mandates for Task Force Eagle was to reduce the volume of weaponry in MND (N), to concentrate what remained, and to conduct periodic inventories so that the collection neither increased nor decreased. It was a task that often engendered some tension between the U.S. forces and the ethnic military organization being inspected.

Not every encounter with the general population of Bosnia was confrontational. Inventorying weapons caches, separating the former warring factions, and securing the zone of separation between them also included identifying and clearing thousands of minefields in the area. With the exception of maintaining checkpoints and aggressive patrolling throughout the area of operations, no other issue so dominated the concerns and actions of U.S. military personnel. Indeed, some military authorities regarded land mines as a greater threat to U.S. personnel than the former warring factions. Others regarded this situation as the most stressful aspect of the Bosnian experience: "You never know when somebody's going to step on a mine."

Bosnia was peppered with at least thirty types of antitank and antipersonnel mines, which were responsible for nearly one-third of all UNPROFOR casualties. Both mine maps and signage were either incomplete or nonexistent, primarily because the inexperienced personnel used to seed the fields with mines did not bother to plot what and where the devices were positioned. The situation became more complex as front lines shifted, and each opposing force laid new minefields or overlapped existing ones. Estimates made after three years of warfare suggested that more than 750,000 mines were in over 30,000 areas.

Photographing Minefields, *by Col. Gary N. "Butch" Cassidy, 1998*

One Army engineer, who had arrived in Bosnia during the first week of JOINT ENDEAVOR, recalled that initially only four minefields were marked in MND (N) and that over the next three weeks he had identified 2,000 more in the same area. By the end of the first year in Bosnia, with over 4,000 minefields known and marked, Army personnel concluded that only half of all the mines in the American sector had been located.

Sweeping for mines

Predeployment training regarding mines and booby traps had been intense and thorough, but accidents still happened—often in a thoughtless or unguarded moment. A typical episode occurred when Army engineers accompanied a Bosnian Serb officer to investigate a mine explosion in an area that had been declared cleared of mines. As they approached the area, their Bradley vehicle struck an explosive device and was disabled. A lieutenant immediately jumped off the vehicle to investigate the damage, in the process detonating an antipersonnel mine; he was thrown into the air and landed on an antitank mine that, fortunately, failed to explode. In another incident, when a military vehicle traveling on a hard-surface road used daily struck an antitank mine, Army engineers learned that the former warring factions occasionally placed

28

land mines under asphalt roads. The former warring factions knew this, and simply assumed that everyone else was familiar with the practice; IFOR personnel had to learn from experience. The lessons from these episodes were inescapable. The danger was omnipresent and could not be ignored. Extreme fluctuations in the temperature, snow and ice, and small alterations of the land surface could obscure the presence of land mines or cause some that had been dormant for years to become active.

The former warring factions were responsible for removing the mines that they had planted. It was laborious work, often made more difficult because few minefields were marked and many had been created or enlarged by different military units and ethnic factions. IFOR monitored most of the mine-clearing operations, but this oversight proved problematic at times. For example, the former warring factions also contracted out mine-clearing tasks to nongovernmental organizations, and these agencies rarely reported the quantity or location of the mines that were removed.

Besides these conventional explosives, Bosnia was littered with booby traps. These devices were usually located in the doors and windows of abandoned houses. Sometimes small explosives were placed inside innocuous objects, such as soda cans or paper bags, and left in public areas for passing civilians to pick up. One civilian was killed when the jacket that he retrieved from a roadside exploded. Though infrequent and few, these random incidents continued for years. As late as 1998 Task Force Eagle continued to encounter explosive devices secretly placed in homes, automobiles, or public buildings.

In addition to concerns over land mines and booby traps, IFOR personnel also contended with infrequent gunfire and explosions. The very random nature of a shot fired in the darkness of night or an explosive thrown from a speeding vehicle only increased tensions within communities and among soldiers. Eventually, occasional sniper fire became less common than the quickly hurled hand grenade, which was "the weapon of choice to settle disputes" among the ethnic factions. And, even four years after the Dayton Accords had been implemented, such violent acts continued to occur.

Although the former warring factions cooperated in identifying the locations of known minefields within the zone of separation, they were incapable of marking all of them. As an alternate resource, IFOR personnel soon learned that local farmers could be equally helpful because in some instances they had planted crops around and through such areas. Nevertheless, the rising number of deaths and the gradual

The experimental Panther used for mine-clearing operations

influx of returning refugees forced Task Force Eagle personnel to conduct mine-awareness classes for the indigenous population. Comic books were among the more popular instructional handouts used to warn children (and adults) about the dangers of land mines and how to recognize them.

U.S. military personnel engaged in some mine-clearing operations, relying upon mechanical methods, visual inspections, and dog teams. The principal proofing method was the experimental Panther, a remote-controlled armored vehicle with the chassis of an M60 tank. Equipped with two five-ton rollers, the vehicle simply drove over areas with the intent of either detonating mines or certifying that none was present. As a "proofing vehicle," it was effective. But this technique did not always work, and occasionally an area would have to be cleared again if a land mine were discovered or, more often, detonated. Military dog teams usually were less effective and were used sparingly before being returned to USAREUR. In many cases, however, the former warring factions were responsible for clearing minefields from the zone of separation, using their own military personnel or contractors. Yet given the slow pace of mine-clearing operations, the unstable nature of many mines, the unknown location of many minefields, and the shear volume of explosive devices, IFOR personnel calculated that it would take another twenty years before all the mines in Bosnia had been removed—"that's if they don't go out and emplace anymore," opined one Army engineer.

The ethnic animosity that afflicted so much of Bosnia-Herzegovina during these years remained profound. By July 1996 conditions in MND (N) seemed less tense, and some political observers speculated that the peace enforcement operation might end later that year. But many others were less hopeful. That month, a young girl with a severe head wound was taken to a hospital in the Serb Republic of Bosnia. While in the operating room, the surgical staff learned that she was a Bosnian Muslim and had her removed from the hospital. Struggling with her open wound, her family was able to move her to a U.S. medical facility, where an Army surgeon completed the operation. The little girl lived, but the episode punctuated the intense hostility that still existed and the near-certainty that the IFOR mission would not conclude anytime soon.

The incident also underscored a recurring difficulty that beleaguered IFOR, particularly Task Force Eagle. The objective of this operation was peace enforcement—not humanitarian assistance or nation building. And yet, many civilians in Bosnia, as well as international relief agencies and nongovernmental organizations, expected U.S. forces to engage in a variety of civic action activities, to include rebuilding schools, roads, and bridges, and providing food, clothing, and medical care. To be sure, Army civil affairs units engaged in such tasks, sometimes as a component of a larger mission requirement and sometimes on the initiative of an individual unit. For example, within the first ten months of JOINT ENDEAVOR, Task Force Eagle assisted the U.S. Agency for International Development with initiating 126 projects that covered various reconstruction efforts and community improvements. Overall, civil affairs units coordinated or organized over 500 reconstruction and relief projects throughout northeastern Bosnia. Several individual units also engaged in relief activities, usually distributing materials that were donated by soldiers or sent from community service organizations in the United States. A typical response was the donation of clothing and school supplies for 800 orphans, which one unit historian regarded as "one of the most important events of the year-long deployment." But these efforts had to be balanced against IFOR's larger security mission and portended the ubiquitous "mission creep" that had bedeviled U.S. forces in similar deployments.

To meet IFOR's requirement for safe travel roads, Army engineers repaired and opened for traffic more than half of the roads as well as over sixty bridges in Bosnia. Task Force Eagle staff officers identified other minor reconstruction initiatives as training missions for engineers, and they often had them funded with materials donated by relief agencies or the local citizenry. Thus, many technicians and specialists provided assistance in restoring public utilities, upgrading communications, and even teaching classes; however, such tasks always were subject to other mission requirements. Notwithstanding the tandem pressures of American soldiers wanting to do more and local civilians and relief agencies expecting additional assistance, the United States and its NATO allies were not in a position to fund or staff many humanitarian tasks. Simply enforcing the Dayton Accords and the overall peace in the region kept IFOR's plate full.

Characteristic of the U.S. Army's involvement in the internal affairs of Bosnia-Herzegovina was the increased security and limited logistical support for national elections in September 1996. This task included a greater military visibility through conducting more patrols, guarding polling places, and escorting the delivery of ballots to and from polling places. Army civil affairs units worked closely with several government organizations to keep the elections on schedule, despite the controversy over which contractor would supply ballot boxes: Serbs rejected a Turkish agency, Croats objected to a Greek company, and no one wanted firms from western Europe. Eventually, the ballot boxes came from Taiwan. The elections themselves were successful, but produced no surprises and largely reaffirmed the intense ethnic and cultural divisions within the country. Nevertheless, the added security precautions and the past ten months of IFOR's peace enforcement operations seemed to have worked. In the words of one Army engineer: "Contrary [to] all expectations, the election was peaceful and boring."

Even before the JOINT ENDEAVOR deployment was completed, planning began for the relief force that would replace the 1st Armored Division in Bosnia. This force, comprising elements of the 1st Infantry Division, was to be ready for deployment by the end of the year if the U.S. government decided to extend the IFOR mission. Extending the mission was a delicate issue, and one that the

Army approached carefully. The president had promised Congress that U.S. forces would be in Bosnia for only one year, but it had become increasingly apparent that neither the IFOR tasks nor the provisions of the Dayton Accords would be fully accomplished before the end of that time period. An extension was almost certain, but only the president had the formal authority to acknowledge this. But despite the uncertainty, specific training began in July with MRE Mountain Eagle III, which spanned three months and embraced two command post exercises, a field training exercise, and individual qualifications training.

To ensure a seamless force reduction and redeployment, the Army ordered the 2d Brigade, 1st Infantry Division, to Bosnia as a covering force for the redeploying Army units. The first brigade elements began to arrive in October 1996. The term *covering force* was necessary at this time, because no public decision had been made about extending the U.S. mission into Bosnia. One month later, following the U.S. national elections in November, the president announced that the mission in Bosnia would be extended another eighteen months, and a resolution of the UN Security Council redesignated the Implementation Force as the Stabilization Force (SFOR). By then the 1st Infantry Division had assumed control of Task Force Eagle, with its 3d Brigade subsequently relieving its 2d Brigade, and by the end of the year the Army had reduced its strength in Bosnia from around 18,500 to about 10,500 soldiers. In the latter half of 1997 the 2d Armored Cavalry deployed from the United States to relieve the 1st Infantry Division of its mission in Bosnia. But even after one year the job for Task Force Eagle would not become easier.

Operation JOINT GUARD

Operation JOINT GUARD officially replaced Operation JOINT ENDEAVOR on 20 December 1996, when the Implementation Force became the Stabilization Force. Having established a firm military presence for peace enforcement operations, the intent of the U.S. contingent within SFOR was to draw down its total force commitment in increments, eventually reaching a baseline of about 5,000 American soldiers by the projected end of the SFOR mission in June 1998. Keeping a highly visible force in such a rugged country while progressively making it smaller was a Herculean feat for Task Force Eagle as it accomplished its assigned objectives and sustained its operational tempo.

The change in command brought a change in mission. Whereas the IFOR mission had been to *implement* the peace, the SFOR mandate was to *stabilize* the peace. IFOR had established and maintained the zone of separation, located and destroyed weapons systems, identified minefields, and created safe travel routes. With a new and much smaller force deployed into the country, SFOR was to maintain the zone of separation, to monitor civilian movements, to oversee the removal of mines, and to inspect weapons sites. More civic action projects and humanitarian assistance programs were also scheduled, including additional mine-awareness instruction for the civilian population.

Early in Operation JOINT GUARD, as though to underscore the future tone of SFOR activities, Bosniac refugees attempted to resettle in a Bosnian Serb area not far from Brcko. The effort failed. An ethnic Serb mob attacked and severely injured one Bosniac who was trying to construct a prefabricated building, and other civilians were threatened. As a result, SFOR personnel had to remove the Muslims from the area to ensure their safety. The Bosnian Serbs burned the unoccupied buildings. The successes of JOINT ENDEAVOR had not altered the hearts and minds of the ethnic groups in Bosnia, particularly in such strategically sensitive areas as Brcko. This small town on the Sava River, seized by Bosnian Serbs early in the civil war, was the only land link that connected ethnic Serbs to the east and the west.

The tensions between the ethnic groups thus remained and sometimes became violent. Random acts of vandalism and isolated outbursts of anger occurred without any identifiable pattern. These episodes usually included throwing stones at passing vehicles, breaking windows, or making obscene gestures to another ethnic group. Occasionally, however, more serious flare-ups occurred that involved direct responses from Task Force Eagle.

The town of Brcko, which was strategically important to the Croats, Muslims, and Serbs, was an especially sensitive site in MND (N). Originally a multiethnic municipality, Bosnian Serbs early in the conflict had seized and fully "cleansed" the town and the Croats and Muslims at the end returned and reoccupied portions of it. U.S. forces were often called upon to quell disturbances, but in late August 1997 a series of incidences escalated into full-scale rioting. Task Force Eagle eventually was able to control the situation, but only after two U.S. soldiers were seriously injured. As a result of this episode, and a concurrent one south of the town, U.S. forces in Bosnia received nonlethal weaponry for riot-control situations and the appropriate training in their use.

Sentry at "Mud" Govern, *by Col. Gary N. "Butch" Cassidy, 1998, depicts SFOR duty near Camp McGovern on the outskirts of Brcko.*

These public outbursts often had the support of ethnic lead-ers. The sponsoring government or a quasi-official government agency generally supplied transportation, usually buses, and occasionally even food and a small stipend to participants in a demonstration. For example, when radical Bosnian Serbs tried to inflame public sentiment in a series of radio broadcasts during August and September, U.S. military personnel attempted to seize the transmission towers. In response, several hundred Bosnian Serbs arrived at the sites in buses to thwart the U.S. forces. A favorite tactic of all the ethnic factions was the employment of large civilian groups—often called "rent-a-mobs" by NATO personnel. In this case, SFOR personnel were able to persuade the Serb authorities to tone down their rhetoric, and the crowd dispersed. When the Bosnian Serbs reneged on their promises weeks later, Task Force Eagle quickly returned in force. The pres-ence of armored vehicles in the predawn hour discouraged the armed guards at the transmission towers from resisting occupa-tion and neutralization of the communications facility, and the speed of movement did not allow sufficient time to organize and bus a mob to the site.

Regrettably, SFOR could not respond to every exigency quickly or with sufficient force to prevent acts of violence. In one notable episode in the spring of 1998 Croatians suddenly massed in a border village that had been resettled by Bosnian Serbs. Several dozen residences and vehicles were burned or damaged. A Canadian unit in SFOR responded once the violence began, but it lacked sufficient force to overwhelm the Croatians. Although there were no fatalities, the incident underscored the fragile ethnic relations that still existed in the country.

For the U.S. Army, the new stabilization mission had begun with a limited timetable as a contingency mission for USAREUR, with small supplements from other active Army and Army Reserve units and personnel. By the latter half of 1997, how-ever, it had become apparent that the U.S. mission in Bosnia-Herzegovina would be extended again and that it would become an Army-wide operation. Perhaps indicative of a probable exten-sion was a congressional appropriation for permanent billets to house almost 6,500 soldiers in that country. In December the president thus announced that U.S. troops would stay in Bosnia beyond the previously set departure of June 1998. Several months later, and viewed by many as demonstrable proof of a much longer U.S. military presence in Bosnia, a 10,000-square-foot multiservice post exchange was opened at the main Army cantonment known as Camp Eagle.

Operation JOINT FORGE

Operation JOINT GUARD officially ended on 20 June 1998. The new military operation, JOINT FORGE, began at the same time, albeit as an open-ended commitment to support NATO and the peace enforcement task in Bosnia-Herzegovina. USAREUR continued to serve as the Army service component command providing oversight for the mission, but in the following years other major non-USAREUR organizations assumed the Task Force Eagle mission in Bosnia. Ranging from six- to twelve-month tours, these units included elements from the 1st Cavalry Division, the 10th Mountain Division, the 49th Armored Division of the Texas National Guard, the 3d Infantry Division, the 29th Infantry Division of the Virginia National Guard, the 25th Infantry Division, the 28th Infantry Division of the Pennsylvania National Guard, the 35th Infantry Division of the Kansas National Guard, and the 38th Infantry Division of the Indiana National Guard. In January 2003 MND (N) was redesignated Multinational Brigade (North), and the total U.S. troop commitment fell below 1,400 military personnel in the area of operations.

Despite the reduced military profile, SFOR was kept busy by almost daily confiscations of weapons, routine patrols, and reactions to either ethnic clashes or tasks that fell within the purview of an expanding mission. The massive amount of munitions that continued to be seized from unreported bunkers, hidden caches, and small improvised arsenals indicated that all three of the ethnic factions might simply be waiting for the peacekeepers to leave before restarting their civil war. To discourage the random acts of violence and vandalism, quick-reaction teams provided security for public ceremonies and major transportation facilities. Mine-clearing operations among the former warring factions continued, and Task Force Eagle sponsored several civic action projects to rebuild the country's infrastructure. Individual and unit training became routine, but served to reinforce the SFOR presence in Bosnia-Herzegovina.

By late 2004 the entire U.S. Army personnel strength fell to less than 1,000 soldiers. Although the Stabilization Force was obviously becoming significantly smaller and assuming a much lower profile, its mission could not be eliminated. Even after nine years of peace enforcement operations, the conditions in Bosnia-Herzegovina posed problems that defied a definitive military solution. The United States, its NATO allies, and several other contributing nations had successfully stopped the civil war, and the widespread killing, horrific destruction, and ethnic cleansing that had shattered the land a decade earlier were over. Roads could be repaired and buildings could be reconstructed. Yet the time when any semblance of ethnic harmony and an unsupervised and permanent peace could return to Bosnia was not in sight.

Thus, on 24 November, when Task Force Eagle officially closed its base in Tuzla and was disestablished, European Union forces assumed responsibility for the Bosnia mission—now code-named Operation ALTHEA. At this juncture, military formations from Finland became the dominant peace enforcement organization in the former Task Force Eagle area of operations. A small U.S. contingent, however, remained primarily as a transition security force to ensure that NATO units could reenter rapidly if the need arose.

Summary and Analysis

The peace enforcement operations—JOINT ENDEAVOR, JOINT GUARD, and JOINT FORGE—were atypical military campaigns. In the spectrum of armed conflict, political and diplomatic issues significantly influenced the Army's actions and created an inverted role in which the absence of fighting was the measurement of success. The U.S. Army, trained to fight, used its resources to avoid conflict, to minimize confrontation, and to keep the peace. It did its job well. Bosnian casualties plummeted with the arrival of the Implementation Force, and IFOR/SFOR casualties were fewer than the respective number for either the civilian populace or the opposing paramilitary groups. Not one American soldier was killed by hostile fire.

However, there were problems. Random acts of violence and vandalism continued throughout the peace enforcement operations, albeit with a gradual decline in their frequency over the years. Although the Dayton Peace Accords called for the free movement and settlement of all ethnic groups and refugees within Bosnia, very few people were able to return to and resettle in their former homes or communities. With rare exceptions, the ethnic groups consistently and categorically thwarted the efforts of those who attempted to move from one ethnic-dominated enclave into another. The former warring factions may have been war-weary, but all three ethnic groups continued to stockpile munitions in anticipation of renewed hostilities. The secret arsenals, illegal weapons, and pervasive land mines kept IFOR/SFOR personnel constantly busy—and vigilant. The

The ever-present sign of danger

peace was maintained, as one brigade commander ruefully observed, "partly because the sides want peace, but also by cajoling, coaching, and outright compelling peace." It was difficult work.

In addition to the seemingly regular confiscations of weapons and munitions, Task Force Eagle continued to wrestle with the complex problems of identifying and removing the thousands of booby traps and land mines that littered the landscape. Thirty months after the first American tank crossed the Sava River the U.S. Army reported that 45,000 land mines had been removed (only 9,000 of them by the former warring factions), yet the database it compiled from various sources indicated that some 116,000 land mines were left. Nevertheless, with so many undocumented minefields, some either adjacent to or overlapping others, the Army estimated that only a fraction of the total number of land mines had been removed. In MND (N) alone, rough estimates suggested that the total number of land mines—documented and undocumented—actually hovered somewhere between 300,000 and 350,000 individual explosive devices. In an uncharacteristic understatement, one Army after action report simply concluded: "Mine clearance, at the current rate, could go on indefinitely."

Yet the tasks were made manageable by the superlative training and preparation that preceded the deployment of successive Task Force Eagle units and soldiers. On several occasions veterans returning from Bosnia commented on how demanding their predeployment training had been and how closely it paralleled their actual experiences. A battalion commander claimed his personnel kept repeating, "This is just like 'Mountain Eagle.'" Others thought that headquarters personnel back in Europe had been hiring Bosnians to replicate past training exercises because the scenarios were simply too familiar. One platoon leader had high praise for the training he and his men received before their deployment, but whimsically added that trainers could not have anticipated everything, "such as an old lady falling into your barbed wire or a farmer who's irate because your tank has torn up his road." Perhaps the one significant shortcoming of the predeployment training was the inability to work closely with units that were later attached or that arrived from other major commands. This disconnect in integrated training was especially true for reserve-component elements that joined IFOR from stations in the United States.

Unlike other campaigns in American military history, the Bosnia operations created an environment in which company-grade officers were directly involved every day in actions that could have strategic implications. Other IFOR participants were amazed that the U.S. Army would entrust captains, lieutenants, and noncommissioned officers with authority and responsibility in various scenarios that could permanently alter the operational tempo and adversely affect the peace in Bosnia. The Army was aware of this great responsibility placed upon junior leaders and tailored its training accordingly. Citing as a typical example of both its successful training and the quality of its small-unit leaders, an after action report noted an episode following ethnic riots in the tense community of Brcko in August 1997. Observing fifteen buses leaving the city, a lieutenant—on his own initiative—followed with his small patrol. Soon, the buses stopped, and 400 people disembarked. Many were inebriated and agitated, showing no signs of purpose or direction in their activity. The patrol halted near the group, and the lieutenant approached the crowd. Immediately, his translator ran away, and the crowd surrounded the young officer. His patrol readied itself for a confrontation. Calmly, the lieutenant asked if anyone in the crowd could speak English, and a man stepped forward. In the interview that followed, the lieutenant learned that the crowd was hungry and fatigued. While admitting that he could not feed or house the large group, he promised to speak to their civilian authorities to seek help. This attention pleased the crowd, which cleared a path for the lieutenant to rejoin his patrol. The lieutenant returned every hour through the night to provide updated information for the crowd. What could have become an international incident became a typical and otherwise for-gotten episode in a NATO-sponsored peace enforcement operation.

And—on the slightly humorous side—there was the story of the American patrol that inadvertently established its roadside checkpoint across the border in Serbia. The soldiers were kept busy all day, leaving Serbian drivers puzzled until the local U.S. commander discovered the error and hustled the Americans back into Bosnia.

JOINT ENDEAVOR, JOINT GUARD, and JOINT FORGE were career-defining experiences for many of the IFOR/SFOR soldiers. The multinational effort behind these peace enforcement operations represented NATO's first out-of-sector deployment, deemed to be a success by all participants. Yet the tenuous cease-fire in Bosnia continues only because of the presence of the NATO-sponsored peace force. As one brigade commander affirmed, "When some-body sees U.S. Army soldiers' boots on the ground, it shows a level of commitment that goes beyond any other level of commitment. People know that we're here to stay, that we're here dedicated to a purpose and dedicated to an accomplishment of a mission. That is not lost on local civilians."

More importantly, peace enforcement in Bosnia may have been a harbinger of future military operations. In waging modern wars in the twenty-first century it no longer is enough to simply win the battles and go home. Given the multitude of ethnic diversity in many geographic areas around the world and the complex issues that engender conflicts among ethnic groups, the U.S. Army may be called upon to engage in more peace enforcement operations. And these require more time and patience. Like major surgery, the operation may be quick but the recovery extremely lengthy.

No one challenges the assertion that the IFOR/SFOR presence in Bosnia-Herzegovina kept the peace in that troubled country, but a meaningful and lasting resolution may be much further away. Peace enforcement operations are not mechanical exer-cises that permit precise planning or exit strategies. As one U.S. Central Intelligence Agency analyst observed, "The flames had been damped down and covered over, but beneath the surface seismic faults and tensions remained." With the stand-down of Task Force Eagle in November 2004, conditions today are certainly better than they were a decade earlier, but there are still people in Bosnia who nurture past grievances and who may seek to resolve them in the future. Until the ethnic groups are able to enforce their own peace, the outside stabilization forces must remain.

41

Further Readings

The civil war in Bosnia-Herzegovina and the events that followed certainly were the most extensively covered political-diplomatic-military issues in the late twentieth century. Thousands of articles, hundreds of interviews, and dozens of books have presented not only the larger analysis of the Balkans and the rise and collapse of Yugoslavia but also the very specific history of Bosnia. It is not possible to list every available source, and neither is it even possible to cite all the better ones available to the general public. Nonetheless, the reader who wishes to pursue a broader and deeper understanding of the issues that led to the peace enforcement operations JOINT ENDEAVOR, JOINT GUARD, and JOINT FORGE would do well to consider the following sources.

Bennett, Christopher. *Yugoslavia's Bloody Collapse: Causes, Course and Consequences.* Washington Square, N.Y.: New York University Press, 1995.

Bildt, Carl. *Peace Journey: The Struggle for Peace in Bosnia.* London: Weidenfeld and Nicolson, 1998.

Burg, Steven L., and Paul Shoup. *The War in Bosnia-Herzegovina: Ethnic Conflict and International Intervention.* Armonk, N.Y.: M. E. Sharpe, 1999.

Daalder, Ivo H. *Getting to Dayton: The Making of America's Bosnia Policy.* Washington, D.C.: Brookings Institution Press, 2000.

Holbrooke, Richard. *To End a War.* New York: Random House, 1998.

Malcolm, Noel. *Bosnia: A Short History.* Washington Square, N.Y.: New York University Press, 1994.

Nation, R. Craig. *War in the Balkans, 1991–2002.* Carlisle, Pa.: U.S. Army War College, 2003.

Silber, Laura, and Allan Little. *Yugoslavia: Death of a Nation.* New York: Penguin Books, 1995.

Swain, Richard M. *Neither War Nor Not War. Army Command in Europe During the Time of Peace Operations: Tasks Confronting USAREUR Commanders, 1994–2000.* Carlisle, Pa.: U.S. Army War College, 2003.

A small archival collection of unclassified after action reports and related memoranda, as well as 300 oral history interviews and a lesser number of draft transcripts, are in the custody of the U.S. Army Center of Military History, Washington, D.C. A larger archival collection is located at the Army Heritage and Education Center, Carlisle Barracks, Pennsylvania. In addition, more detailed monographs about the U.S. Army's peace enforcement operations in Bosnia and the Balkans region are being prepared by the Center of Military History, the U.S. Army Europe, and the U.S. Army Special Operations Command.

www.ingramcontent.com/pod-product-compliance
Lightning Source LLC
Chambersburg PA
CBHW081128280526
45787CB00007B/3012